About the Author

This is Mar McKenna's debut book. From a very young age, they have practiced writing creatively. As the years progressed, they found themself drifting toward poetry as their major art form. As *Time Walks By*, includes the poems they have written that they deemed the best of their works from 2020 through early-2022.

As Time Walks By

Mar McKenna

As Time Walks By

Olympia Publishers
London

www.olympiapublishers.com
OLYMPIA PAPERBACK EDITION

Copyright © Mar McKenna 2023

The right of Mar McKenna to be identified as author of
this work has been asserted in accordance with sections 77 and 78 of
the Copyright, Designs and Patents Act 1988.

All Rights Reserved

No reproduction, copy or transmission of this publication
may be made without written permission.
No paragraph of this publication may be reproduced,
copied or transmitted save with the written permission of the publisher,
or in accordance with the provisions
of the Copyright Act 1956 (as amended).

Any person who commits any unauthorized act in relation to
this publication may be liable to criminal
prosecution and civil claims for damage.

A CIP catalogue record for this title is
available from the British Library.

ISBN: 978-1-80439-284-3

This is a work of fiction.
Names, characters, places and incidents originate from the writer's
imagination. Any resemblance to actual persons, living or dead, is
purely coincidental.

First Published in 2023

Olympia Publishers
Tallis House
2 Tallis Street
London
EC4Y 0AB

Printed in Great Britain

Dedication

To my parents: Thank you for everything.

Acknowledgements

Firstly, thanks to all my friends who have given me unconditional support. Even at my lowest points when I have been willing to give up, you all kept encouraging me. Without all of you, this book would likely not exist. Thank you to my 10th Grade English teacher, Mrs. Hawley, as well. You helped me find the bravery to share my writing with the world. To my favorite writing buddy, my dog, Julie, thank you. I know you can't read this book, but you're my favorite company when I write. And lastly, thank you to everyone else who has helped me along this journey. Without every one of you, I wouldn't be here today.

The Gift That Nobody Asked For

The gift that nobody asked for
Lies under the tree.
Nobody will wonder what it is,
But they'll wonder why it is.

And they'll never understand.
They'll beg that the gift isn't real.
But it's there,
Wrapped in blood.

I didn't ask for the gift either,
But we all get
Gifts nobody asked for.

We both had to unwrap layers of pain.
We both wish we were free
From the
Gift that nobody asked for.

Stand

Stand.
For respect.
Respect for a man who won't look you in the eye.
Respect for a country with apathy towards you.

Stand.
Without thinking.
Thinking leads to questioning.
And we can't allow that.
Thinking will lead you astray.

Be pressured
To stand.
Pressure that will eat at us all until
We stand.

Your pressure won't eat at me though.
Your pressure won't make me follow your commands.
I won't stand for your inanimate objects,
And I certainly won't
Stand for you.

Amen

To muffle the cries of distress just outside,
Amen.
To put a mask over a differing identity,
Amen.
To prove oblivion,
To have no consequences,
Amen.

Allow the word to ring through the halls.
Allow the word to reside in your mouth.
Comfortably.
Permanently.

Amen.

The Bullets

Grasp my hand.
Hold it tightly
As you dodge the bullets away.
But,
I feel your fingernails.
They dig into my hand.
Pain worse than the bullets.
Pain that's constant.
The pain of betrayal.

You can't keep it safe.
You can't keep your promise.
Leave me with the bullets.

Hieroglyphics

The hieroglyphics.
That scar.
The art that cuts like a knife.
They reveal who I am.
They reveal my crime.

The hieroglyphics.
That display everything I try to hide.
That are my cry for help.
Will be covered up.

Nobody gets to know
My secret.
Nobody gets to know
What the hieroglyphics mean.
Nobody gets to see me.

We'll all ignore the hieroglyphics.
We'll ignore the art.
They'll go away
If nobody knows.

Free but Average

Stand in the crowd.
Stand in the back.
Applaud.
Never to be noticed.
Never to be special.
Never to excel or to be your family's joy.
Just average.

Free from all the expectations.
Free from all the stares.
They can't pass judgment;
They don't know me.
Just average.

Like everyone who's come before,
And everyone who will come after.
Another face in the swarm.
Another unmentionable face.
Just average.

Free,
But average.

Heavy

Heavy hangs the head where the heart lies.
Heavy, as the heart pleads with the head
More pressure.
More work.
More worth.
The pressure builds up in the head.
As the heart
Begs for more.

Heavy hangs the head where the heart lies.
Heavy as the heart sympathizes.
But the head can't take any more.
But the heart is in pain.
But they all need your ears.

As the head becomes heavier,
And the heart continues to grow,
So does the throne.
And the pedestal because they can't see the weight.
They don't see that.
Heavy hangs the head where the heart lies.

Paint Me a Picture

Paint me a picture.
Of a Utopia.
Let me live there.

Paint me a picture.
Of a future.
Just out of reach.

Grasp for it.
Grasp for the light.
But the chill of the night air
Stings my face.

The rain falls,
But I see the light.
I see the rainbow.
I'll be there.
I promise.
And I'll join your harmonies.

Heat

The heat melts my skin.
And I can't breathe in the ash;
I'll suffocate.
The sizzle burns my ears.

"Help,"
But he gets on one knee.
I say yes,
And the ring of fire melts my finger.
Before spreading to my body.
But I said yes.
Now I'm stuck with him.
Now I'm stuck with the pain.
And the heat that melts my skin.

Cottage Fairy

Play me a tune,
Cottage Fairy.
I'll listen to your voice float above the meadow.
Every string you pluck is the sound of angels.

Grant me a wish,
Cottage Fairy.
Give me the medicine to halt my heart's throb.
I know you can help more than a doctor could.

I'll hide in the forest.
And listen to your tunes.
I won't ever ask anything from you.

I won't clip your wings,
My worst fear of all.
I'll stand behind you,
Keep you standing tall.
You will never see my fall.

Smoke

Smoke your cigar.
Smoke away fifty thousand dollars
After you send them away.

They needed help.
They needed school,
But you killed them.

Smoke your cigar.
Smoke away fifty thousand dollars
As their bunker blows up in smoke.

Smoke away,
And they will too.
Bond with them over that smoke.

A looming smoke that burns their brains
And only burns your ashtray.
But you are the same.

You,
With the green you sit upon
And them,
With the green they hide in.

The Ice

The ice will never melt over this frozen oasis.
The summer warms the ice,
But it will not melt.
The heat,
Combined with the ice,
Makes it seem like a miracle.
But it's not.
It's a deadly combination.

The ice,
It begs you to slip,
And taunts you,
Being water just out of reach.

The heat,
It strips you of hydration.
And laughs as you beg for safety.

You hope for warmth in the oasis,
But you were only taunted.
Only distressed.
Only killed.
By the warmth of the oasis.

Spark

The fire burns as bright as the sun,
But the spark isn't there.
We still had to set up our logs.
We still had to start a fire,
But the spark was never there.

The fire will burn long into the night.
Long into the day,
But our fires contain the same oxygen.
There's only one difference:
Our spark was never there.

Pool of Blood

Swim in a pool of blood,
Just barely making it to the other end.
"It's not that deep."
"I've swam in more blood."
But did you know who's it was?
Did you see their slaughter?
I did.
And I still swim in blood.

Your Freedom

I will be your freedom.
Your wings cannot be clipped forever.
Your voice cannot be silenced for eternity.
As you sit in your gilded cage,
Look outside.
I will be there.
I will be your freedom.

When there's no song left in your heart,
When the light in your eyes has faded to gray,
Look outside.
I will be there.
I will be your freedom.

One day,
I will show you blue skies.
I will tame the sun so you never lose hope.
I will be all I can.
But I won't be all you know.

Until that day comes,
Look outside.
I promise to be there.
I promise to be your freedom.

A Marriage

That walk down the aisle
To prove your love to those who don't care.
To prove you are one.
And you are tame.
The wolf has become a dog.

The ring on your finger.
The shackles of tradition.
Tradition enforced to put you on a leash.

Walk on your leash.
Wear your shackles.
And they'll never see the foaming at your mouth.
They'll never see it when you rip your leash to shreds.

Hurt Me

Strangle me.
I can't breathe as it is.
An excuse will help.
If they see the marks,
If I have a story to tell,
They'll understand.
Survivors aren't weak.

Stab me.
When I shudder at a knife,
They'll sympathize.
I didn't cause my own pain.
And I have the scars to prove it.

Hurt me.
Torture me.
In any way you can.
Let them all see my pain is justified.
I can be hurting.
Can they see?
Not unless I have the scars to prove it.

Destroy My Home

Destroy my home.
And I'll fly away.
They'll swim through the oil.
We'll all leave.
We don't need to be here.

Destroy our lives.
For profit.
For wealth.
Your wealth means much more than our lives.
We are objects
Used for profit.

Take away all we know.
For all you will ever know.
And move on.
To destroy another home.

Build Me a Road

Build me a road,
And we'll walk it together.
Never mind how long.

As our feet grow weary,
And as our eyes lose their sparkle,
I look into yours,
And I remember why I'm here.

Build me a road.
I will guide you around potholes,
And the hills don't scare me.

As long as I walk with you,
Our road can continue forever.

Waiting

Like a kid on Christmas Eve,
I sit at the gravesite.
Waiting.
That hole will be filled.

I wait for the gift,
Wrapped in a black box,
To be lowered down.

I sit here for decades,
Hoping my gift will arrive today.
I sit here for decades,
Hoping my gift will make it soon.

I can tell it's mine from the packaging.
Don't try to fool me.
I will always know,
So I continue to wait.

The Surprise

There's a surprise hiding behind the flesh.
A surprise that you can see.
A flesh prison you can tear away.
Tear away the prison trapping the surprise.

The sharpest tool.
The sharpest tool allows a bigger surprise.
Quicker.

The surprise will thank you,
As it rises to the surface.
It will call out your name as it floods out.
But you grow weak,
Pained,
Pale.
As the savior becomes a corpse,
You'll know what the surprise is.
As it all fades to black.

Ruin Our Friendship

Ruin our friendship,
Run away.
I'll hold you in my arms,
And we'll be together.
Forever.

Ruin our friendship.
I've wanted to do this for so long.
We belong together,
But not as one.

Ruin our friendship.
I'll hold a knife in my hand.
Until I rest your corpse in my arms:
With your body in my backyard,
We'll never be separated.

We have to ruin our friendship.

Only One

Only one,
But I'm free.
Roam the world with one suitcase.

The stained white t-shirt.
The messy hair.
I look like Apollo.

He criticizes my hair.
And she tells me about washing machines.
But I am Apollo.

"Not mature."
"Waiting on the right person."
But am I?
I am one,
But am I
Only one?
Was Apollo waiting on the right person?

Fabricated Heart

My heart has been sewn.
I thought it had a beat.
I thought it was like yours,
But my heart pumps cotton.
Not blood.

My heart isn't real.
Should I have a transplant?
Should I pretend it's real?
Should I destroy it completely?

Who made my heart?
It's still missing a piece.
I'll never know a heartbeat.
I'll never know blood.

Lone Survivor

Since tomorrow may not come,
Let me write your name now
When the ink of white you were stains their brains,
They won't forget.
They can't forget.

Because tomorrow would be a miracle,
Let me review your face once more.
To make sure I'm not the lone survivor.
The lone survivor who forgets.
To make sure if we fall,
We fall together.
Not just aside each other.

Tomorrow is forever away,
But you're right here.
And I promise to not let them forget us.
They won't forget you.

Feel Something

Let me feel something.
Let my fingernails be nubs.
Nubs that will bleed out.
And as my face turns a sickly white,
I am a clown.

A ghostly white face,
Highlighted with a giant smile,
Hiding the darkness in my brain.
A bright yellow sunray I shine on the world.

Let me feel something.
Don't pity me when you see my bloodshot eyes
Or the tears staining my cheeks.
They mean my heart still beats.
They mean my brain still thinks.
They work together to feel something.

Let me feel something.
So my heart,
So my brain,
Have a chance of climbing out of their abyss.

Cobblestone

As we walk side by side,
I see our roads hold different rocks.
Both hold cobblestone
And are laced with emeralds.

But yours are more frequent.
But yours are brighter.

Tears sparkle too
To make up for my lack of emerald.

But the gray is calming.
Grounding.
I don't need more sparkle.
And don't break my cobblestone.

Today and Tomorrow

Give me a needle today.
So tomorrow,
I can recognize the face in the mirror.
So tomorrow,
My bags from nights of crying are gone.
So tomorrow,
Everyone will know who I am.

Give me a cut today.
So tomorrow,
I won't agonize over who I don't know.
So tomorrow,
I won't drown in a sea of my own tears.
So tomorrow,
I will stop begging to not wake up.

Give me a needle today,
Or tomorrow might not come.

Today I Killed God

Today I killed God.
There were no cries of agony,
Nor shrieks of mourning
As I left his castle in the sky.

Today I killed God.
I killed the monarchy looming over the afterlife.
I killed oppression for those who should rest.

I have yet to face his wrath.
I have yet to meet the Devil.
I have yet to hear a single complaint because
Today I killed God.

Eagle and Mouse

Pierce the sky.
Soak up praise
As you soar by.

A little mouse,
So desperate and alone,
Fly down.
Make him feel at home.

He begs for his life
As you grab him with your talons.
And you place him in a bush,
But all you've done is make him shushed.

Rips in his stomach.
Rips along his back.
A chance to survive
Is what he lacks.

Praise yourself
As you fly away,
And his whole world turns gray.

Death and Life

If death came to my porch,
I would not cry,
He knows best.
I wouldn't be in pain.
I'd follow him home.

If life starts on my porch,
I'd grab my gun.
He loses his light as every second draws on.
Why shall he lurk around doing nothing?
Why shall he continue to stay around?

Why is death late?
I've been patient.
I've been waiting.
But I have to wait.
Wait until life fades.
Completely.

Let Them Bleed If They May

Let them bleed if they may.
My hands are free of blood,
Mine and theirs.
Blood was inevitable.
But their blood will mix.
And nobody will remember.

Let them bleed if they may.
But when you trace the blame,
Forget me.
I fired no shot.
Forget me like you forgot them.

When the poppies start to grow,
You'll be glad.
I let them bleed.

The Flame

The flame rises from within.
And they try to extinguish it
With kind words.
With praise.
With their threats.

I've never seen a death
Caused by your threats.
And I've never seen life
In your eyes.

The flame burns brighter
With every word you say.
It will burn you down.

And as you look at your own ash,
Do not pity me.
It was inevitable.
A flame has to fight water first.

Teach Me Everything

Teach me everything.
From your finger size
To your blood type
To the feeling of your eyes.
They have encapsulated me
With their ice blue color.
I must encapsulate them.

Teach me everything.
We can grow closer than we ever have.
Nobody else knows the taste of your liver.
Nobody else has your tongue in a drawer.

Teach me everything.
Maybe it will hurt.
But I promised to be with you
In better and in worse.
Be patient with me.
As I learn everything.

Quiet and Peaceful

Quiet.
Peaceful even.
But the mockery.
And the twisted trees.
They reflect their sinister intentions.

Return, peace.
Return, quiet.
Fall from Earth.
Peel back humanity.
Peel back realism.
And see the galaxy before us.
The stars shine a message of hope.
Hope that his face will be visible.

But.
Nothing gold can stay.
Nothing worth having will last.
And the blood rises in my mouth,
Spilling out the eyes.
Drowning in them.
Never to be quiet.
Or peaceful.
As the forest returns.

Rage

Rage boils
As I hear his screams.
A sound that relentlessly fights me.
Fights my sanity.
Won't it go away?
But as I ignore him,
The screams get louder.
One day,
I'll be sane.
But until then,
Constant pain.

Stay

Please be alive.
Please survive.
When I wake up,
Where will you be?
On Earth with me?
Or somewhere else,
Unable to hear my pleas?

Don't you see that I love you?
Don't you see that he loves you?
Don't you see that we all love you?

Please,
To awake without you would be tragic.
Please,
To awake without you would be devastating.

Stay,
If not for you,
For me.
If not for me,
For him.
If not for him,
For her.
For all of us,
Stay.
It will get better.
I promise you.
But only if you stay.

I See

I see the colors that blanket your life.
I see the pain throbbing in your heart.
A gentle soul.
A kind soul.
Don't tell me it doesn't feel.
Don't tell me it's made of stone.

I see the claws brought upon you.
And I continue to hear a lack of screams.
The shadow man shouldn't have to cry for your help.
The shadow man can't always rescue you.
Don't tell me, "It's fine."
Don't tell me, "Not to worry."
I see too much.

It's Not Mine

It's not mine.
Every time I look at it,
I see your fingerprints.
I see the scars you left
And I'm reminded
It's not mine.

I try to run from you,
But you always find a way back.
Sneak in through the windows of my mind.
Sneak in to every moment.
And consistently remind me
It's not mine.

Let Me See Our Future

Let me see our future.
Because love is a science.
Let me do my lab work.
So I don't have to think with my field experiments.

Let me finish my studies
Before I make any rash decisions.
Maybe if I know how to feel,
I will feel that way.
You will not have an unreciprocated love.

Let me see our future.
So I know how to act.
To be happy.
To make you happy.

The Knife Downstairs

Let the light flicker out.
And stare at a ceiling reflecting hope
Reflecting guilt.
"It's your fault."
"All your fault."
But there's a knife downstairs.

Let your disguise wash away.
Look at who you are.
Who you'll always be.
No changing it.
But there's a knife downstairs.
Dissect your insecurities.

Let my heart start to thud.
And my breath starts to quicken.
Never to survive a day.
The voices keep shouting.
But there's a knife downstairs.
End the anxiety.

End it all.
The pain.
The suffering.
Let all your soul spill out on the floor
From the knife downstairs.

Time Keeps Running

Time keeps running.
Whether it's manageable or not,
It will keep running.

And when it's gone,
We're never enough.
We fall short.
We fall flat.

And when we're gone,
Nobody will remember us
Because time keeps running
Without us.

I Can Swim

Try to scream,
But your voice is too hoarse.
Try to cry,
But not a tear is left to shed.
Try not to ask for help,
But not a word will come out.

Give me a life raft.
Please.
But I can't ask.
And I can't accept.

Watch me drown,
And beg me to grab the life raft.
But I can swim.
As the waves splash above my head,
I can swim.
As every breath becomes shallower
And fills my lungs with water,
I can swim.

But one day,
I'll never come up for a breath.
Even then,
I can swim.

Heart Over Heart

We watch the heart beat.
As ours do too.
Hand over hand.
Heart over heart.

But the blood will be shed.
The screams will be heard.
My heart will be pierced.

But the knife cannot last.
The pain always will though.
The visions always will.

Still,
For the time being,
Hand over hand.
Heart over heart.

Lawfulness

Follow the rules.
Or at least try.
Don't ever step out of line.
And don't ever catch yourself wondering why.

To be yourself,
The true tragedy of the phase.
To be yourself,
Will not provide a living wage.
To be yourself,
Nobody will care.
So sit down.
Sit back.
And never share.

My World

Come to my world.
Maybe you'll finally understand.
Please understand.
See what I see.
But what I see would scare you.
I'll hide that in the closet upon your arrival
Because I couldn't bear to see your discoveries.

Lurk

The shadows lurk.
They'll lurk in subtle ways you'll never see.
They'll always be there though.
Whether you see.
Whether you refuse to see.
Whether you don't see.
They'll always lurk.

Suffocate

Suffocating.
The sound of my own name.
Suffocating.
I can't breathe around them.
They know who I am.
It leaves me
Suffocating.

Let me breathe,
But I shove my face in a pillow.
But I won't let you know why I can't breathe.

Suffocate.
Suffocate.

It'll kill me.

Our Game

Play pretend.
Pretend like you know me.
Pretend like I know you.
Pretend like we don't know the truth.

And when our game ends,
All our scars will be revealed.
And the truth is much more bitter than our game.
So keep your mask on.
And I'll keep mine on.
And our game never has to end.

No Real Problems

Drown out my cries in a sea of laughter.
It's just a joke.
No real problems.

Not scars parading themselves around in glitter.
It's just a joke.
No real problems.

Not the same sobs you hear every night,
Only from a different source.
It's just a joke.
No real problems.

No real problems until you see,
Which you never will.
So there will never be
Real problems.

Real Boy

Be the puppet.
You were designed to be their toy.
And you'll continue to hear their reassurance:
"You're a real boy."

But,
If you were,
Why do they throw you away
When you move by yourself?

They'll bring you back eventually
If you're lucky.
If you didn't move too much.
They'll hope you learned.
Don't move.

Real boys don't move.
They'll run with their kites, though.
While claiming you're real,
Like they are.

Are they even real though?
Or are they puppets of their own minds?
Of the illusion of power we've given them.
The only difference is
Nobody stops them from moving.

Sunray

You shine down your light.
It warms me.
But that was never your intent.
But you never will mean that.

I'll let your sunlight shine down from a mile away.
I promise not to infringe on it.
I won't absorb all the light.
I know you need it.
To cloud your sunlight would be a crime.

Sunshine is a gift.
You deserve it though.
You are the ray of sunshine
That brightens my day.
My sunray.

You Don't Know Me

You don't know my name.
And you seem so confident in what you say
But you can't hear my pain.

You don't hear my silent tears
Or my rants about my millions of fears.
My feelings aren't clear,
And I know I shouldn't feel so queer.

But, you don't know me.
You don't know how I feel when you call me she.
You don't know how I feel about, "Us girls… we."
You don't know me.

And one day, maybe I'll break free.
Until then, you don't know me.

Leaf Juice

The tea will get cold.
The milk will spill.
Another pot to be boiled.
Another mess to clean up.

And without the warmth to remind you of the joy it brings,
You drink leaf juice.
Cold.
Bitter.
Leaf juice.

With the milk dispersed on the kitchen floor,
You're reminded:
It wouldn't make anything better.
To soften your troubles,
To bring you light,
But no matter how much you add,
It's still
Cold.
Bitter.
Leaf juice.

Stay put.
If there's no tea to be made,
There's no disappointment to be had.
No faith placed in the milk to restore your tea.
No cold, bitter, leaf juice.

The Little Orange Bottle

The little orange bottle
Keeps me stable.
It keeps my heart
One hundred beats per minute.
It keeps the knife out of my hand.
Out of my wrist.

The little orange bottle
Keeps me social.
It masks my desire to take a gun on every person.
And then myself.
It hides the screams of the world.
And my brain.

The little orange bottle
Is my life.
It keeps me alive.
It lets me survive.

All I live for is
The little orange bottle.

Come Nightfall

It's a different place
Come nightfall.
Everyone is asleep,
But He is always awake
Come nightfall.

He owns the night,
Spreading jelly on their beds
Come nightfall.

How Many Times

How many times
Do they look at me
And see an object?

How many times
Have they wanted to hurt me
Because they find me attractive?

How many times
Have they told me to show more
Even though I don't want to?

How many times
Do people deal with this
Every day?

The question of
"How many times?"
Should be zero.

But,
How many times
Must it happen
Until it's at zero?

The Birds

Listen to the birds.
They are gone. They won't return.
One day, that's you too.

It

It taps on the glass.
Cover your heads.
You can't see it then.
It can still see you.
It can always see you.

It's All on Me

It sticks to my skin.
It shows my stomach.
It's time to go change because
It's all on me.

It's not only their looks;
It's their hands.
It's the clothing.
It's all on me.

It's not, "Don't objectify her,"
Or,
"It's harassment" because
It's all on me.

When I ignore him,
When I ask him to stop,
When he's the one inflicting pain,
It's all on me.

Blind with a Gun

It was me.
I loaded the gun.
Even though my eyes were closed.
I encouraged him to shoot you.
Right in the back.

We were blind.
We didn't know a bullet could kill you.
And yet—
Your blood stains the carpet.

The thought of you lying there,
Unable to move,
Unable to breathe,
Swarm my head like angry bees.
I should scoop out my brains
To rid myself of the bees.
I can't though.
I won't.

Have I fired more guns?
Was I blind to the aftermath?

It was me.
The one who pulled the trigger
Would have no ammo if not for me.

Not a Cult

Not a cult.
No pain is inflicted.

"Burn the gays!"
"Burn the Muslims!"
"Burn the feminists!"
"Burn them all!"
"They're all witches!"

Not a cult.
No pain is inflicted.

Cattle

We trudge along
Like cattle.

Find a buddy!
Find a friend!
Because maybe loneliness allows us to realize
We're cattle.

All the distractions to prevent us from knowing
We're cattle.

Better than them?
Smarter than them?
At least the cattle knows he's not free.

At least the cattle gets to go
To the slaughterhouse.
The farmer only whips us our whole lives.
Then we die.

Maybe we're worse off
Than cattle.

In Broad Daylight

Tied up
In broad daylight.

Given chloroform
In broad daylight.

There are no screams,
No blood,
No trace of my body
In broad daylight.

An efficient killer
In broad daylight.

I See Their Smiles

Like a sea full of plastic,
I see their smiles.

Awkward conversations,
Lacking a bond,
And yet,
I see their smiles.

"So sad to see you go!"
"Great friend!"
"I love you!"

What's my name?
Who am I?
I'm just another smiling face.
Just another one to bring up your reputation.

Don't pretend.
I know the lies.
I know who you are.
I know who I am.
Don't act like we're friends
Because I don't tolerate pity.
I don't tolerate their smiles.

Trapped

Trapped in a cage.
Trapped in a schedule.
Trapped down my path.

"Good little girl!"
"Just like us!"
"The key to happiness."

How is that the key to happiness
When I'm
Trapped?

God is Dead

God is dead.
Folding their hands together,
Their eyes now red,
He doesn't hear.

God is dead.
Begging for food
Without a crumb to be spared,
He doesn't care.

God is dead.
Their bodies scatter like leaves,
Their bodies that once knew how to bleed.
He "doesn't know."

Does he work for the rich?
Is he their bitch?
Does heaven cost a fee?
That we refuse to see?

Does God bow down to their will?
That idea is shrill.
Or is God dead?
Unable to do a shred?

Ignore Me

Don't see me;
I don't mind.
Leave me be;
We'll both pretend to be blind.

But don't plaster on a smile.
And act like our friendship will last a while.
Don't live in denial.
Don't act like our personalities are the same style.

We can still act nice,
But we don't have to roll the dice.
Or fall down the rabbit hole.
Neither of us have to change our mold.
Together, we don't have to grow old.

Till

'Til be wouldn't die today,
We must fight.
'Til his death says more about the past
Than the present,
We're not equal.
'Til they would be held accountable,
Has much changed?

Try as we might,
The blood will never wash off our hands
From the death of Emmett Till.

One Day

One day,
The struggle will dissolve.
One day,
This will mean nothing.
One day,
Nobody will remember
Our names,
Our faces,
Or why we died.

I'll remember though.
I'll remember you.
I'll remember your passion,
Burning inside you like a flame of red.
Burning for the illusion of freedom.

Take my hand.
I'll give you the illusion.
And one day
Will never come.

Pretending

The piano drowns the cries.
Pretending,
They no longer exist.
Pretending,
The piano saves lives.
It's her cry.
I know the cry.
And soon,
The others will follow.
Before my chance to say goodbye.

Berry

I spent the summer with him.
He gave me warmth.
He gave me comfort.
And abandoned me,
And left his family
Who can't love like he does.
He called himself Berry,
But I can't find him.
My Berry.
My strawberry.

I Drown

Bring me joy.
Give me satisfaction.
As I see your speckles,
I drown in euphoria.
I drown as I pronounce your name.
You bring me serotonin.
You bring me dopamine
As you stand there,
Growing in the forest.

Lion and Mouse

Stuck in their echo chamber.
An echo chamber voicing the roars of lions,
Not the mouse.
Even when the mouse knows better than them.
Who can hear her squeak?

Suffocate her.
Silence her.
Scare her into the corner.

If you kill all the mice,
Will you be happy?
Maybe your freedom is an illusion.
Maybe where we're not all equal,
None of us are free.

The Bodies Lie

As gunfire turns to the chirps of the birds,
The bodies lie.
As poppies begin to grow where they once fought,
The bodies lie.
As children ask about that fateful June night,
The bodies lie.
And as another group of naive
Hopeful
Young
Revolutionaries rise up,
The bodies lie.
One thing prevents their fighting:
The reminder that
The bodies lie.

Slit Our Wrists

A cult.
Slit our wrists.
We bleed red, white, and blue.
Slit our wrist for a man
Who claims to bleed red, white, and blue.
But he has no scars.
And his doctor says he bleeds green.

I bleed red though.
I won't slit my wrists for him.
I slit my wrists to escape him.
Once you see my blood on your flag,
Will your blood turn red?
Or will it remain multicolored,
And deepen,
Seeing I ruined your flag?

Death's Hand

He took my hand
And spun me across the floor
As we danced toward a new life.
For I never knew love
Until I took
Death's hand.

He pointed toward the pool and said,
"Look."
I was him.
We were the same.
I never knew freedom
Until I took
Death's hand.

He let me rest as I need.
He let me do as I please.
He gave me inner peace,
Which I never knew
Until I took
Death's hand.